KT-226-455

What's the Point?

Text copyright © 1986 Norman Warren
This edition copyright © 1999 Lion Hudson

The author asserts the moral right
to be identified as the author of this work

A Lion Book
an imprint of
Lion Hudson plc
Mayfield House, 256 Banbury Road,
Oxford OX2 7DH, England
www.lionhudson.com
ISBN-13: 978-0-7459-4133-2
ISBN-10: 0-7459-4133-8

First edition 1986
10 9 8 7 6 5 4 3 2 1 0

All rights reserved

The text paper used in this book has been made from wood
independently certified as having come from sustainable forests

A catalogue record for this book is available
from the British Library

Typeset in 11/12 Venetian 301
Printed and bound in Malta

What's the Point?

Finding answers to life's questions

NORMAN WARREN

LION

Contents

What's the point?

'Jim worked hard all his life. He'd just retired and we were looking forward to enjoying ourselves – now he's dead. What's the point of it all?'

'We brought this child into the world. He goes his own way – never says thank you – now he's in trouble with the police. What's the point of it all?'

'I've been married two years. We were saving up to get our own place. I thought everything was fine – now my wife has cleared off with another bloke. What's the point of it all?'

'I've worked hard at school, got my qualifications and can't find a job. What's the point of it all?'

'It took us eight years before we could have a child and now our little girl has got cancer. What's the point of it all?'

'The way things are going we are destroying our world. What's the point of it all?'

'I go to work, come home, eat, sleep, go back to work. Life is one dreary bore. What's the point of it all?'

What is the purpose of life – why am I here?
Is there a God and does he care?

Who am I?

There is so much about life that is unreal and dreamlike. Moments come when we find ourselves asking the questions:

- Who am I?
- What is life all about?
- Why am I here?

I feel so small and insignificant, and wonder deep down

if I matter. In the eyes of the state I am just a number, one among many millions. How can I be of any importance?

I look in the mirror and am sometimes startled by the stranger who seems to be staring back at me.

I am alive – I must be – I go to work, I talk to people, I eat. I go to bed and sleep, and then wake up the next day. It all suddenly seems so pointless and empty. Time rushes by. Birthdays come and go and I wonder where the years have gone.

Where do I fit in all this? I seem to be going nowhere fast.

The universe is so vast. The endlessness of space is so frightening. Even our Earth looks a mere speck as we hear of stars and galaxies millions of light years away. Yet here on Earth for the first time in human history we have the ability to blow it and everything in it to pieces. The whole thing seems like a sick and senseless joke.

We go to the funeral of someone we know, killed on the road. We hear of a friend struck down with cancer in the prime of life and we suddenly think, 'That could be me.' We wonder if there is anything after death – or is that the end of me?

Most of the time we try to sweep all these thoughts away as we slip back on to the merry-go-round of life with all its passing attractions.

But the fears and aches and uncertainties will not go away. All the time they are still lurking just below the surface.

What is the purpose of life?

*All I want is to be happy. As long as I have a home, a family and friends, and enough money to do *what* I like *when* I like, life is good. I'm fine.*

But deep down we know these things do not satisfy. We try to shut from our minds everything unpleasant. We don't want to look too closely at ourselves for fear of what we might find. And so the days and weeks and years of our life drift by with ever increasing speed.

Then some tragedy strikes. You lose your job. A close relationship goes wrong. Someone you love dies and your world comes crashing down.

'Oh God!' we cry out, but we are not sure if there is a God who hears or cares, and we feel lonely and empty.

The happiness we long for vanishes like the morning mist.

This book has been written so that you can know that there is a God and that he does care for you and has a purpose for the whole of life that is slowly and surely being worked out.

How do we know there is a God?

Some people say, 'There isn't a God because I can't see him.' There are many things in everyday life we cannot see, yet we know they are there.

We cannot see the wind. We know it is there because we can see it blowing the washing on the line and the leaves in the trees.

We cannot see electricity. We know it is there when we switch on the light.

We cannot see air. We know it is there because we couldn't live for a minute without it.

We cannot see love. We know it is there in those who care for us.

We cannot see God. We know he is there because of the wonderful world all around us. It is full of beauty and colour and amazing designs, from the tiniest insect to the vast, unending universe.

Things do not happen by chance. With a book, the words

do not fly through the air and happen to land in the right order. Someone has to put it all together to make sense. So a book must have an author: someone to write it. A painting must have an artist: someone to paint it. A building must have an architect: someone to plan it.

So too with our world. It did not all happen by chance.

Someone planned it, put it together. This great Designer, Architect, Creator, we call God.

Who made God?

God is the name we give to the great and wonderful Creator: the one who made the whole universe, the one who alone gives life.

We live in time, so we have a beginning and an end, our birth and our death. Because we are like this we think that God must be like this, too.

But he is different. The Bible tells us God has no beginning and no end. He is not limited by time – hours, days, weeks, months and years – as we are.

If someone had made God, then that someone would have to be greater than God. But God is all-powerful, almighty. Who made God? Answer: no one.

Think of space. It has no beginning and no end. God is eternal: he has no beginning and no end. He is far greater than our little minds can ever take in.

We live in a world of change. Fashions changes, politicians rise and fall, heroes of sport and the music world are at the top one year and are forgotten the next.

We change too: our friendships, our habits, our bodies.

God never changes. His love and care never change. He doesn't love us one day and ignore us the next. He is the only one we can trust who will never let us down.

No one made God. He has always been there. He never changes. He never grows old or weak.

What is God like?

By studying a book or a piece of music you can discover something about the person who wrote it.

By looking at creation and the world in which we live, we can learn something of the Creator. We can see that the Creator loves beauty and colour. We can detect his care for the tiniest detail. He is a master engineer and architect. The working of the human body is a masterpiece of design and function.

The size and power of the mountains and seas and the vast distances of space all tell us something about the almighty power of this Creator God.

But what is God like? To know him for ourselves we have to wait for him to reveal himself to us. We can discover what God is like in the Bible. He tells us that 'God is Spirit.' But what does this mean?

We have a body for living here on earth. A fish has a body for living in the sea. God lives in heaven, so he is Spirit.

This does not mean that God is an eerie ghost. He has a will and a mind. He is able to be everywhere, see everything, know all that is going on. He is able to love us, guide us and protect us. He is far too wonderful for us to understand fully.

So he decided to come in person to our earth and show us what he is like in a way we can understand. He came as a baby. His mother was a country girl called Mary.

He was born as we were – and yet his birth was different because God was his Father.

Jesus was fully human – and yet he was also fully God. He

was a normal human being, but he was also God, living among us

Because he is human he knows the sort of problems we face
Because he is God he is able to help us.

Jesus said, 'He who has seen me has seen the Father.'

How did it all begin?

Scientists tell us that it took millions of years for our earth to be as it is today. They can work out the age of the rocks fairly accurately. But when we turn to the Bible and to the first book Genesis, we are told that the world was made in six days. Isn' this all a glaring contradiction in terms?

We must remember that the Bible is not a book on science and it is not written in scientific language. In fact, the Hebrew word for day can mean not only twenty-four hours but also an age or period of time. So when we read Genesis chapter I we can see the story of creation in a new way. We can see not just *how* it happened, but *why* it happened.

Behind all the activity in creation we see God slowly but surely working out his plan for all living things.

But what was his purpose and why are we here?

We have been made in God's likeness. This does not mean God has a huge human body. It means that, like God, we are able to love and choose, to think and make rational decisions We have a mind and a will. We have been made to have a specia relationship with him: to know him and love him, to belong to him and be his children.

We have been made to worship God. Even the most primitive man has this inbuilt desire to worship a god.

We have been made with very great creative skills in music art, science, medicine and engineering. It is in our very nature to invent and explore. Where we see all these skills being creatively used we see God at work, whether he is acknowledged or not. For he is not only the giver of life in all its variety and richness, he is the very source of life.

What has gone wrong?

Everything about the world God had made was good. There was plenty of food and drink for every living creature. In this lovely setting the first people lived.

God wanted them to be his friends and look after the earth and everything in it. God gave to them a precious gift: free will. He did not make them like robots or machines so that they would have to love him and obey him. It is impossible to make someone love another person. Love must come freely and naturally.

The gift of free will was one of the main differences between humankind and the animals. It meant that men and women could choose between right and wrong, good and bad. They could choose to love each other or not. They could choose to love God or not, to do what he wanted or what they wanted, to live for God or for themselves.

Sadly, they chose to disobey God. They preferred to please themselves rather than God.

Why did they do this? What went wrong?

All evil and wrong come from the devil. Even the very word 'devil' has the word 'evil' in it. While everyone today believes that evil exists, belief in a personal devil has declined. Isn't he just a comic figure with horns and a curly tail?

The Bible tells us to take the devil seriously. It tells us that, far from being a comic figure, he was once a glorious angel in heaven. His name was then Lucifer, which means 'one who bears light'. He became proud and jealous, wanting to be like

God. He was banished from God's presence and now does all he can to turn men and women against God.

It was the devil, or Satan (a name which means 'the deceiver') who tempted the first man and woman to choose wrong and disobey God.

So it was that sin and wrong entered into our world and so into human life.

It is the devil who has gone on tempting people away from God right from the very beginning.

Because people listen to the devil's lies, they go his evil selfish way. It is this that causes all the crime and wrong and suffering in the world. This is why there is so much evil, so many broken relationships, so much selfishness and greed.

We are all by nature self-centred rather than God-centred. It is a disease we all have and it affects not just us, but everyone we come into contact with.

The Bible calls this 'sin'.

This is what is wrong with the world, and that means you and me.

Why do we do wrong?

Why is it that we all find it easier to do wrong than right? We don't have to teach children to be selfish and naughty; it just seems to come naturally, and we have to teach them to be good.

There is within every one of us a desire to do what we want. Evil and wrong are there in the life of every single person born into this world. We see it in all the hatred and violence, the selfishness and broken relationships in the world. The news on radio and television is one never-ending list of all this. We see it as people stand up for their rights regardless of others. We see it as we look at our own lives, if we are really honest with ourselves.

We all want our own way, and this is what the Bible calls 'sin'.

Many people do not like the word 'sin' and try to think up nother. So they call it faults or failings. You can change the abel, but you can't change what is inside. For a chemist to emove the label 'poison' and replace it with another is not only oolish but very dangerous. The Bible keeps to the true label, 'sin'.

Sin is not just killing, stealing or telling lies and ommitting adultery.

I sin when I do what I want, when I want my own way. This s the root cause of all our troubles, unhappiness and quarrels.

I sin when I cannot be bothered with God. He has made me nd given me everything I have: my health, my body, my mind, ny abilities. I didn't give any of this to myself. I belong to God vho gave it all to me. I sin when I say: 'I'm the boss of my life – t's mine – I can do what I like with it.' This is sin.

I sin when I do not love God with all my heart. Jesus said he greatest commandment of all was: 'You shall love the Lord our God with *all* your heart and with *all* your soul and with *all* our mind. This is the first and greatest commandment.'

Not one of us has loved God like this. We have all broken he greatest commandment. We are at heart self-centred rather han God-centred.

This is the real problem with us all.

Why is the world in such a mess?

What we do affects others. Kindness brings happiness to other eople, while selfishness will result in misery and pain.

The Bible wisely says that whatever we sow we will also reap.

My own self-centred nature does not only affect my life, it vill also have an effect upon all I come into contact with.

Sin spoils. Sin is like an ugly blot on a clean page. Being selfish, lazy, thoughtless, telling lies and dirty stories will not only slowly ruin your own character, it will also poison other people's. So often we just do not realize how much what we say and think and do affects others.

A drunken father will bring untold unhappiness into his home and seriously damage the lives of his family. A selfish 'I'm always right' attitude will quickly destroy the happiness of a friendship or marriage.

▌*Sin spreads.* Sin is like weeds in a garden; if not rooted out they will soon overrun it. Quite small acts of dishonesty can so soon spread into attitudes and habits we cannot break. That first drug fix will almost without our realizing become a prison we cannot escape from. One harsh word, if not followed by an apology and forgiveness, can make a relationship sour and strained.

▌*Sin separates.* Worst of all, sin separates us from God. Sin is like a thick cloud which blots out the sun. This is why God seems to be miles away. He is very near, all around us, but sin acts like a great barrier between us and God.

See that car – a good engine, plenty of petrol, but it won't start. Why not? Dirt in the spark plugs.

Sin acts like this between us and God. He is pure and holy. He hates sin, but loves us. Our sin blocks the way to him. God longs to make himself known to us, but he cannot, because sin gets in the way.

What has God done about it?

What can we do about it? Answer: nothing. We cannot remove the barrier ourselves. We cannot get through to God on our own.

The Bible uses some vivid pictures to describe our situation.

We are chained up in a deep dungeon with no way out.

We are sinking in thick mud: the more we struggle, the worse it becomes.

We are lost, like someone aimlessly wandering around in a maze getting further and further from the way out.

We are drowning and we do not know how to swim.

Being sincere, even being religious and doing religious things is no help either. What is the answer?

We need rescuing. We need someone to unlock the dungeon, someone to lift us out of the mud, someone to find us and take us home, someone to rescue us from drowning.

Showing us what to do is no use. Nor is telling us what to do any better. We need a Rescuer.

God in his love has not left us to struggle hopelessly. He has done something about it. He has sent someone to rescue us and his name is Jesus. The name means Saviour or Rescuer.

The Bible explains it like this: 'God so loved the world that he gave his only Son so that whoever believes in him should not perish but have eternal life.'

Here is the proof that God does love us and he does care. He came himself in the person of Jesus Christ. Jesus said that he came to seek and save the lost. He did not come just to show us what God is like. Nor did he come just to teach and live a perfect life. He came to save us, and this meant losing his own life to rescue us.

But did Jesus really exist?

Some people ask whether Jesus ever really lived. Wasn't he invented by the first Christians?

There are good reasons to believe that Jesus was a historical person. He actually lived here on earth. He was born in a small town called Bethlehem in Israel at a time when the country wa occupied by the Romans.

The very existence of the Christian church shows that Jesu lived. Millions of Christians down the centuries have claimed to know and love Jesus and have been changed by his work in their lives.

The Bible points to the reality of Jesus. The four gospels Matthew, Mark, Luke and John, were written by people who either knew Jesus personally or who had first-hand information. Many of their stories give us eyewitness accounts of the life of Jesus.

Secular historians such as the Romans Pliny and Tacitus who lived at the turn of the first century, describe what the first Christians were like: the followers of one Jesus, crucified under the Roman Governor Pontius Pilate and who is said to have risen from the dead. Pliny was very disturbed because the Christians 'prayed to Christ as to a God', and because of this the pagan temples were being deserted as more and more people became Christians.

Josephus, a Jewish historian, who also lived at this time and who had no love for Christianity, describes in detail Jesus' life and teaching, his death and the reports of his resurrection as indisputable facts. He writes of Jesus as a wise man who did marvellous deeds.

Jesus certainly was historical, but what was he really like?

What was Jesus like?

Jesus was fully human. He was born of a human mother. He grew up in a family and spent his early years working as a carpenter in a small village. At the age of thirty he began his teaching ministry, wandering through the towns and countryside of Israel with no home and no possessions.

He gathered around him some friends, among them a few fishermen and a taxman. For three years he travelled, healing, teaching and caring for any in need. He loved to be quiet and alone in the hills and pray to his Father. Equally he was at home with people and enjoyed being with them. He was able to get alongside all kinds of people, from sophisticated Pharisees to social outcasts like thieves and prostitutes.

He touched lepers and healed every kind of illness. On several occasions he raised the dead to life in full view of witnesses. He ordered evil spirits to leave those who were possessed and so find peace and wholeness in their minds.

His life was one of serving and helping others. There was not one fault in him. He never needed to say 'sorry' or to apologize. There was no stain of self-interest, jealousy or unkindness in him. He demonstrated pure love at all times. True, he was angry, but his anger was justified and perfectly controlled. He was angry at the way God's house was being used for extortion and greed instead of for prayer.

He knew what it was to be hungry and thirsty. On one occasion he was so tired that he slept in a small boat tossed about in a fierce storm. He knew what happiness and friendship were like.

He also knew what it was to weep in deep personal grief and to be deserted by his friends. He experienced rejection and unfair treatment. He went through the most fearful pain when he was mercilessly flogged and then crucified: the Romans' most cruel and painful death. Even Pontius Pilate, the Roman Governor who tried him, admitted he could find no fault in him.

Here was a perfect man in every way.

At first his followers saw him as a great teacher and healer. As they watched him and listened to him, so they slowly realized he was more than just a great man, he was a prophet. More than that, he was God's promised Deliverer or Messiah. And, more than *that*, he was the Son of God: God himself living among us in human form.

So it was that John could write that Jesus 'became a human being, and full of grace and truth lived among us. We saw his glory, the glory he received as the Father's only Son.'

What did Jesus teach?

Jesus came to show us what God is like.

As he met and talked with people, caring for their needs and healing them, he showed what God is like in action. And he also gave us teaching that has been the model for moral standards right down the centuries. One example of this is the famous Sermon on the Mount in which Jesus tells us how we should live if we belong to the Kingdom of God, the rule of God as King in the world.

In two short memorable stories he shows what God's love is like. It is like a shepherd going out after one lost sheep until he finds it. It is like a father whose younger son demands his share of the inheritance. The boy wastes his father's money, realizes the mess he is in and returns home, sorry for what he has done and fearing his father's rejection. But his father is on the lookout and welcomes him with open arms. That, says Jesus, is the measure of God's love and forgiveness.

Jesus was one who was a model for living and teaching: a moral miracle. Yet he said the most staggering things of himself. He insisted on humility in others, lived a humble selfless life himself, and yet he said that he was God himself: 'He who has seen me has seen the Father.' 'I and the Father are one.'

He said that he was able to forgive sins. To a man who was

paralyzed he said openly, 'Your sins are forgiven.' He claimed openly to do what only God can do.

He said that he was the only way to God: 'No one comes to the Father except by me.'

He promised peace to all who come to him: 'My peace I give you. I do not give it as the world does.'

He said that he had victory over death: 'I am the resurrection and the life. Whoever believes in me will live even though he dies.'

I To know him was to know God.
I To see him was to see God.
I To trust him was to trust God.
I To hate him was to hate God.
I To honour him was to honour God.

These breathtaking statements must either be true, or Jesus was a liar, a fraud, a deceiver or just plain mad. But his perfect life and his remarkable teaching show him to be the most wonderful person who has ever lived. This can lead us to the same conclusion that Thomas, the doubting disciple, came to as he fell at Jesus' feet: 'My Lord and my God!'

Why did Jesus die?

We saw a few pages back that what is wrong with the world, and what is wrong with each one of us, is that we have all sinned.

Our self-centredness not only does untold harm to others, it also cuts us off from God, so that he seems to be miles away and not to care.

We cannot get back to God on our own; we are not good enough. What was needed was someone who was perfect, with no sin of his own, who could bring us back to a relationship with God. Before that could happen, the problem of human sin had to be dealt with. We needed someone to rescue us and that is why Jesus – God's Rescuer – came.

If you fall into a river and cannot swim, you don't want someone to give you your first swimming lesson – you need someone to rescue you.

If you get heavily into debt, you need someone to step in and pay the debt and rescue you.

But how can Jesus, who lived and died 2,000 years ago, rescue me from my sins today?

Think of God's character as a coin with two sides: justice and love. Because of his justice, God rightly condemns us, for sin and wrong must be punished. We would not think much of a judge who kept on letting guilty criminals go free.

Because he is love, he longs for men and women to become his friends. It is as though God had a problem: to remain just yet to forgive people who were guilty because of the wrong they had done.

When Jesus died on the cross, God's justice and love were perfectly satisfied. Sin had to be punished, so God in his love sent his Son to die in our place, bearing the death penalty our sins deserved.

This was why he cried from the cross, 'My God, my God, why have you forsaken me?' The full punishment for our sins was taken by Jesus. He was cut off from his Father for us.

Peter was one of the followers of Jesus who watched Jesus die. He wrote: 'Christ died for sins once and for all, a good man on behalf of sinners, in order to lead you to God.'

That is how much God loves you and me. There was no other way that we could be rescued from our selfishness and pride. Just before he died Jesus called out, 'It is finished!' This was not a cry of defeat: 'I've had it!' No, it was a cry of victory, 'I've done it!' The huge debt of our sins was paid once and for all

The way back to God is now wide open, forgiveness of all our sin is freely offered, friendship with God is now wonderfully available for the asking.

Did Jesus really rise from the dead?

> **Someone rising from the dead? Impossible! Once you're dead, you're dead – that's it!**

There was no doubt about it: Jesus was dead. When the Romans carried out an execution they made sure the person was really dead. In fact, one of the soldiers stuck a spear into Jesus' heart just to make sure.

There was no doubt about it: Jesus was buried. A man called Joseph from the town of Arimathea, with a friend, took the dead body of Jesus and laid it in a tomb carved out of rock, presumably reserved for himself. A huge stone was then rolled over the entrance and a guard posted.

Jews and Romans alike all knew Jesus was dead and buried. As far as they were concerned, he was well and truly out of the way. The friends of Jesus knew he was dead: they had seen him die and be buried in the tomb.

The women even prepared spices to anoint the body and went to the tomb on the third day. Then came the terrible shock: the body was gone. The grave clothes were still there, but the tomb was empty.

What happened to the body of Jesus? That is the key question. There was no doubt about it, the tomb was empty. Everyone concerned knew which tomb it was; there could be no mistake about that.

Did the Jewish or Roman authorities take the body? If they had, then they would certainly have produced it when the friends of

Jesus claimed Jesus was risen and alive.

▌ *Did the friends of Jesus take the body?* The tomb was guarded by soldiers and the disciples were frightened, broken people. There is no way that they would later have risked their lives proclaiming Jesus was alive when all the time they knew it was a lie; when all the time they knew where his body was rotting away.

If the body of Jesus was not taken by his enemies or his friends there can be only one possible answer to the question.

God raised Jesus from the dead.

Nothing else explains the many appearances of Jesus. For forty days he appeared to his friends, usually in broad daylight in a variety of places: in a room, on a road, by the sea. Sometimes it was to a single person, sometimes to twos and threes, sometimes to the eleven disciples, sometimes to crowds of them, even to 500 all at once. These appearances cannot simply be explained as hallucinations.

He met them, talked with them, even ate with them. They could see him and touch him. He was no ghost. He was the same Jesus they had seen dying on the cross. The marks of that terrible death were still there on his hands, feet and side. He was the same, yet different. He now had a resurrection body, not subject to time and space.

Nothing else explains the incredible change in the disciples. They had been scared out of their wits, totally disillusioned, complete failures, shattered by the unexpected death of Jesus. But now they became people full of joy and confidence. They went out into the market places fearlessly proclaiming that Jesus was risen from the dead and alive, the conqueror of death and sin.

This was why they knew that Jesus was far more than just an ordinary man; that he was God.

This was why the Christian faith spread so far and so fast and why millions of people from all backgrounds, countries and cultures worship Jesus as Lord.

He is alive, and they know it in their own experience.

What is a Christian?

'I was brought up in a Christian home. My parents always went to church.'

That's good, but that doesn't in itself make you a Christian any more than going to the zoo makes you a chimpanzee.

'I believe in doing good and helping others.'

Quite right, too, but this is not enough to make you a Christian. Many people who don't even believe in God can be kind neighbours, ready to do a good turn to anyone in need. But that doesn't make you a Christian.

'I was baptized when I was little.'

So are thousands who care little about Jesus. Going through a religious ceremony doesn't make you a Christian.

'I believe in God.'

The Bible tells us that the devil does, too! He knows there is a God all right. Most people, if asked, say they believe in God, but have little or no idea who God is or what he is like.

You can believe that a jet travels across the Atlantic Ocean, but you will not travel one centimetre just by believing it. You have to get on the jet and go.

Believing in God, right though it is, is not enough to make you a Christian.

Well then, what is a Christian?

The name 'Christian' was a name given to some of the firs followers of Jesus. It meant those who belonged to Christ Christ-ian: Christ's men and women.

The best description of a Christian comes from Jesu himself. He described Christians as those who have bee reborn.

Each of us has been born by the ordinary, natural processe of birth and so become part of the human family. But we als need to be *born* into God's family if we are to become part o that family. This does not happen by natural means, by bein born into the 'right' family or by doing good or by bein religious. We have to be born all over again, starting a new life We cannot do this on our own; it is something God promise to do for us.

God in his love for us has done everything necessary. H sent Jesus to die on the cross for our sins so that we can b forgiven and become his children. The way is now wide oper There is nothing to stop anyone, no matter who they are o what they may have done, from coming to know God. He ha done his part. And he asks us to do our part.

Do you want to become a Christian and know Jesus Chris in your life?

Do you want to know that he has forgiven all your sins an that you are a child of God?

Do you want to know that you have eternal life, the life o God in you, and that when you die you will go straight to b with him in heaven? If so, read on…

How can I become a Christian?

❙ *Something to admit.* Admit that you have sinned in the sight of

God. Own up to him the many things in your life that you have said, thought and done that you know deep down were wrong. Be truly sorry for the times you have ignored his love and gone your own way. Be willing to turn from every thought, word, action and habit that you know to be wrong.

Something to believe. Believe in Jesus Christ as the one who died on the cross bearing all the guilt and penalty of *your* sin. We all deserve to be punished for the wrong we have done in God's sight. Believe that Jesus took on himself the punishment that you deserved.

Something to consider. Consider that Jesus never promised that it would be easy to follow him. People will misunderstand you, laugh at you, oppose you, just as they did Jesus himself. Becoming a Christian means to accept Jesus as your Lord and Master. This means that every part of your life – your work, your friendships, your time, your money – all must come under his control

Something to do. Accept Jesus Christ into your life to be your Saviour to rescue you, your Lord to control you, and your friend to be with you. So many people miss this last step and so never come to *know* Jesus Christ.

Perhaps nowhere is this step clearer than in the last book of the Bible. In the Book of Revelation (chapter 3 and verse 20), Jesus himself is speaking. He says, 'Listen! I stand at the door and knock; if anyone hears my voice and opens the door, I will come into his house and eat with him and he will eat with me.'

Your life is like a house. Jesus Christ waits outside. He will not force his way in, for that is never the way of love. He wants to be invited in. The door handle is on the inside. Only you can open the door. You become a true Christian when you open the door of your life to Jesus Christ and invite him to come in and to live in your heart and life.

Have you ever done this? Perhaps you have never before realized that there was anything to do. You can be baptized, go to church, even read the Bible and pray, and still leave Jesus Christ outside the door of your life. Face this question honestly.

Is Jesus Christ outside your life or inside? Will you invite him in or keep him out?

You cannot ignore his invitation for ever. Time is fast running out. After death there will be no more opportunities to accept Christ. It will be too late.

If you are ready thoughtfully to open your life to him, find a place when you can be quiet and alone.

Think of Jesus' love for you – the cross, the shame and pain, his body nailed to the cross, his blood shed – all for you.

Think of Jesus knocking now, waiting to enter your life. You have heard his voice and want with all your heart to know him personally.

You might find this prayer helpful if you want to open your life to Jesus and invite him in. Pray it phrase by phrase, quietly, thoughtfully, thinking carefully about what you are saying and doing.

Lord Jesus Christ,
I know I have sinned against you,
in my thoughts, words and actions.
There are so many good things I have not done.
Please forgive me.
I am sorry for my sins
and turn from everything I know to be wrong.
You gave your life upon the cross for me.
Gratefully I give my life back to you.

> *Now I ask you to come into my life.*
> *Come in as my Saviour to rescue me.*
> *Come in as my Lord to control me.*
> *Come in as my friend to be with me.*
> *Thank you for hearing and answering me.*
> *Amen.*

If you have said this prayer and meant every word, you have asked Jesus Christ into your life and he has come. He now lives in you by his Holy Spirit.

If anyone hears my voice and opens the door I will come in.
Revelation 3:20

Jesus is God. When he makes a promise he always keeps it. Don't rely on your feelings. Trust his promise. You are now a child of God, a real Christian. You have been reborn.

To all who received him he gave the right to become God's children.
John 1:12

You now have eternal life.
He who believes has eternal life!
John 6:47

You will never be alone.
You are now a child in God's family, part of his body, the church; all who trust in Jesus whatever their colour, background or intellect.

I am with you always, to the end of the age.
Matthew 28:20

Can I be sure that God has accepted me?

You have opened the door of your life and asked Jesus to come in. You have accepted him. But has he accepted you? How can you be sure? You may not feel any different at the moment. You may not feel you are a Christian. How then can you be certain that Jesus Christ has come into your life and is a living personal friend?

One of the special marks of Christian faith and one of its greatest joys is that God wants us to know for certain that we belong to him and he to us. We can be sure because of three things: the Bible, the Cross and the Holy Spirit.

We will be looking at each of these over the next few pages.

How do I know that I have eternal life? How do I know that Jesus Christ will be with me at all times? Because God says so in the Bible.

The Bible is full of the clear promises of God to all who trust in Jesus. It shows us how to become a Christian; it shows us the way forward. We cannot trust our feelings. If you are tired or ill, or if you have troubles and worries at home or at work, you may not feel you are a Christian. Feelings go up and down, so don't rely on them. Instead, learn to rely on God's promises, which never change.

I *How do I know God loves me?* Jesus said, 'God loved the world so much that he gave his only Son so that everyone who believes in him may not die but have eternal life' (John 3:16). That is how much God loves you; there is all the proof you need. God sent Jesus to die on the cross for you and give you eternal life.

I *How do I know Jesus is in my life?* Jesus said, 'If anyone hears my voice and opens the door, I will come in…' (Revelation 3:20).

If you have asked Jesus into your life, then he gives you some firm promises. He says clearly and definitely, 'I will come in.' Not, 'I may come in if you are good enough.' Don't rely on what you feel. If you have asked him in, you can be absolutely sure he has come in because he says so. God always keeps his word.

I *How can I be sure he will always be with me?* Jesus said, 'I am with you always to the end of the age' (Matthew 28:20). You may not always feel that he is there, and you certainly cannot see him. But he is with you always in every situation, because he says he will be. We can trust the promises he has made.

One of the loveliest promises Jesus ever made was this: 'Everyone whom my Father gives me will come to me. I will never turn away anyone who comes to me.'

You have been given by the Father to Jesus. You now belong to him not just for time alone but for eternity. There is no greater security than this.

How can I know I am forgiven?

Is it really possible to know that every sin, every bad thought, every rotten action, every thoughtless word, every bit of selfishness I have ever done can be forgiven and blotted out?

One of the results of sin is to cut us off from God, which is why he seems distant and unreal and not to care about the frustrations and sufferings of human beings. The trouble with most people is that they think they can bridge this gap by their own efforts. They hope to win favour with God by being kind, sincere, honest and by being religious.

But God accepts us as we are because, and only because, of what Jesus has done and not for anything we can ever do. We can never get through to God on our own. The cross alone bridges the gap between us and God. The way back to God is wide open to all who stop trusting in their own goodness and who put their whole trust in Jesus.

The cross tells us that God will forgive all our sins for Jesus' sake. There in that lonely, painful death Jesus took the full death penalty our sins rightly deserved.

Peter, one of Jesus' disciples, understood this as he wrote 'Christ himself carried our sins in his body on the cross.'

Another disciple, John, also could confidently write: 'Christ himself is the means by which our sins are forgiven.'

Paul could see that the whole judgment of sin had been taken by Jesus: 'There is no condemnation now for those who are in Christ Jesus.'

All who trust in Jesus will not have to face the judgment of God for their sins. The judgment is over. Jesus took it for us on the cross. This was what he meant when he cried out, 'It is finished!' The debt of human sin is paid.

The cross tells us that the enormous debt of our sin has been fully paid by Jesus Christ once and for all. When we accept Jesus into our lives, we receive God's forgiveness. Every sin is blotted out. God promises not only to forgive all our sin but to forget it as well, as though it never happened. John, one of Jesus' followers, wrote: 'The blood of Jesus, God's Son, purifies us from every sin.'

What does it mean to follow Jesus?

The Christian is not one who chooses to follow Jesus, like someone deciding to join a tennis club or even a church.

The Christian is one who has been chosen by Jesus. He said 'You did not choose me, I chose you.'

The Christian has been chosen to be a disciple or follower of Jesus. This means not only knowing him and loving him and trusting him, but it also means being totally committed to him.

This is how Jesus described a disciple: 'If anyone would come after me, he must deny himself and take up his cross and follow me.'

❙ *Deny myself.* Jesus was not talking about giving up sweets for Lent or denying oneself some small luxury. It is something far more radical: saying 'no' to the old self-centred way of living and thinking and saying 'yes' to Jesus. A disciple is a learner, and as a disciple I will want to listen to Jesus and obey him. For my life is no longer mine to do what I like with. It now belongs to Jesus. He is the Lord and master of all that I am and all that I have. I am answerable to him for what I do with what rightly belongs to him.

❙ *Take up my cross.* For Jesus the cross meant pain and shame, loneliness and rejection, suffering and death. Jesus calls his disciples to follow that same path and not to be surprised when misunderstanding and opposition come. Probably more Christians are suffering for their faith today than in any other period of history.

To take up the cross is a picture of personal sacrifice. Jesus on the cross gave his life for us. He calls his disciples to give up their lives to him.

Follow Jesus

The disciple aims to live like his master:

❙ to care for others as Jesus did
❙ to accept people and to love them as Jesus did
❙ to have time for people, especially any in need
❙ to be a light in the world by living a life of truth, honesty and compassion as Jesus did.

Why read the Bible?

The word Bible comes from a Greek word, *biblia,* which means 'books'. The Bible is not just one book, it is sixty-six books. It is in two parts.

The first part is called the Old Testament, with thirty-nine books. This tells the history of God's dealings with the Hebrew nation before Jesus came.

The second part, the New Testament, has twenty-seven books. This tells of the life, death and resurrection of Jesus. It then describes the growth of Christianity and gives practical advice on how to live the Christian life.

The Bible took about 1,500 years to be completed. It was written by about forty people. Among them were kings, a prime minister, a doctor, a taxman, fishermen and a farmer. Most of the writers never met the other writers. Yet through the Bible there runs an amazing unity and agreement. What is the explanation?

God spoke to the Bible's writers and guided them to write down his words ands instructions. They did not just sit down and write what they thought God was like and what God was saying. Again and again we have the words, 'Thus says the Lord' or 'The Word of the Lord came to...'

God did not speak to human word processors. He spoke to men who were in close touch with him. He used their differing personalities and they wrote down God's words in their own way, using their own words.

So John could write: 'What we have seen and heard we declare to you.'

Peter, writing about the Old Testament books, put it like this: 'Holy men of God spoke as they were moved by the Holy Spirit.' (The word 'moved' means carried along, as a sailing boat is carried along by the wind.)

Paul summed it by saying : 'All scripture is inspired by God.

How could the followers of Jesus possibly remember all he said and did? The answer is that Jesus promised them that the Holy Spirit 'will teach you everything and make you remember ll I have told you'.

God made known to these men his laws and his will, and they wrote it down not just for their own generation but for all time. This is why the Bible is different from all other books. Through it God speaks to us today and on every page is his stamp of authorship.

The Bible tells us what God is like and how we can know him. Without it we would know next to nothing about him. We would have no idea why we are here or where we are going. The Bible sheds light on every kind of problem. It speaks with certainty on life and death and eternity. It is our guidebook from earth to heaven.

Is the Bible true? Can I trust it?

It is not just a book of history, yet it is full of historical facts and events that can be verified from other historical sources.

It is not just a book of great literature, yet it does contain wonderful poetry and gripping stories.

It is not a book of psychology, yet it shows a wealth of understanding of human nature and personal relationships that work in practice.

It is not a book of science, though it does tell us so much about our world. Science is concerned with finding out how things originate and work. The Bible is more concerned with answering the question why.

The proof of the pudding is in the eating. The final proof of whether or not the Bible is true is in the reading – and then in following its teaching.

How can I read the Bible? Where should I begin?

The Bible is not an easy book. You will need help and you will need method. It is not a good idea to start at Genesis and work through the Bible. You will very soon get bogged down

among all the laws in Leviticus. Nor is it a good idea simply
open the Bible at random and hope for the best.

Try starting with the Gospel of Mark. Then try Paul's let
to the Philippians, then the Acts of the Apostles, Psalms 1–
and the Gospel of John.

By yourself, you will never understand or enjoy the Bible. *
the Holy Spirit to help you. Believe that God is going to speak
you.

Many Christians find it helpful after reading a Bible pass
to ask such questions as 'What do I learn about God – abo
Jesus – about myself?' 'Is there a promise for me to claim –
example to follow – a warning to heed or a clear command
obey?'

Pick out a verse or a phrase that strikes you; learn it and t
it with you into the day.

Try to set aside a definite time each day when you can be alc
and quiet. Make time to meet with Jesus and to read the Bible.
course, this isn't always possible for everyone, and it isn't a ca
iron rule. But spending time each day can be extremely help
There are no short cuts to success and growth in the Christ
life.

An excellent method of daily Bible reading is to follow a ser
of Bible reading aids. You have a booklet that will give you
Bible passage and helpful comments on it. Your vicar or minis
will gladly tell you about them.

How can I overcome wrong?

◊I know what I'm like – I could never keep it up!◊

When you become a Christian you do not become perf
overnight. Nor does your heavenly Father leave you to mud

along as best you can. You are now a child of God and he wants you to become more like Jesus. For this reason he has given you his Spirit – the Holy Spirit.

The Holy Spirit is not a vague, ghostly creature. He is a person in every respect, except of course he does not have a human body like us. He has a mind and a will. He can love and guide, protect and help. He possesses great power and authority, for he is God. He is all-powerful, all-knowing and is present everywhere.

When you felt a need for God, it was the Holy Spirit prompting you.

When you became a Christian, it was the Holy Spirit who led you to accept Jesus.

The Holy Spirit comes into your life when you open your heart to Jesus. He is Jesus' promised gift to every Christian. Jesus himself is in heaven, but he lives and rules in the lives of his followers by his Spirit.

The Holy Spirit brings to the Christian the calm confidence that he or she is a child of God and in his family. His special work in every Christian is to help them become more like Jesus.

He will strengthen you to overcome temptation and bad habits. You still have your old self-centred nature as well as the new nature God has now given you. It is as though a tug of war is going on inside you. The devil is tempting you to do wrong and to pull you away from God's love. The Holy Spirit is there to help you overcome wrong and stay on God's side. The Holy Spirit is far stronger than the devil and victory is always there for the asking.

Only the Holy Spirit can change human nature and make a self-centred person unselfish and thoughtful.

Only the Holy Spirit can give the power to control the tongue.

Only the Holy Spirit can turn anger and resentment into love and compassion.

He will develop in your life the character of Jesus: his love, joy, peace, patience, kindness, goodness, faithfulness, humility and self-control.

He is always there to guide you in times of difficulty and uncertainty. He will help you to understand the Bible. He will help you to pray. He will lead you to discover God's will and purpose for your life.

He gives gifts and abilities to enable you to serve God at home, in the church and in the world.

His task is to prepare every Christian for that great day when we will see Jesus Christ face to face in our eternal heavenly home.

What about church?

A Christian is someone who has been born into God's family by trusting Jesus Christ. The church is another name for God's family.

The church is not a building. It is a family of people who belong to God here on earth and in heaven. It is a family in which all are brothers and sisters bound together not by flesh and blood but by the Holy Spirit, who gives us love for Jesus and love for one another.

The church is not a sect or denomination: Catholic or Protestant. It is a great worldwide body of people whatever their colour, background or intellect who trust and follow Jesus. There are many local churches, part of the one universal church – Anglican or Episcopalian, Methodist, Baptist, Roman Catholic, Pentecostal – to name just a few.

To be a Christian means you belong to the worldwide

hurch, but also to a local church.

For a Christian to talk about 'going to church' is really rather ridiculous. He or she is already in the church. What is meant of course is going to a local church *to worship God*.

'But must I go to church every Sunday?'

Put the question another way. 'Must I visit my parents or friends?' The answer is, 'No, you don't have to, but you do because you love them.'

The Christian faith is built on love; on a love relationship. God loves us – that is why he sent Jesus. We love him – because he first loved us. We love one another – because we are in God's family and because he has poured his love into our hearts.

If you really want to follow Jesus, you will want to worship God and meet with fellow members of God's family to thank him for all his love and goodness to you.

You will want to show openly that you belong to Christ. Going to worship God each week marks you out as a follower of Christ.

You will want to learn more about him as the Bible is read and explained and so grow stronger in faith.

You will want to join with other Christians to pray together.

You will want to give generously to support God's work at home and abroad.

The apostle Paul said that the church was like a body with Jesus as the head.

There are many parts to the human body: arms, legs, eyes and ears, to name but a few. All are important and all have a special job to do, each dependent on the others. And this is how it is with the body of Christ, the church. Each member is important with a special contribution to make for the proper functioning and growth of the whole body.

This means that every Christian is vitally important to the whole church. No one is unimportant.

What is prayer?

The Christian life is a two-sided friendship. And prayer is the way that our friendship grows and develops.

Prayer is speaking to Jesus about anything, anywhere, anytime. It is to the Christian what breathing is to the human body.

Prayer is your direct link with headquarters, rather like a walkie-talkie, where you can keep in touch all the time. Prayer links you directly with your leader, Jesus Christ. Advice, help and guidance are constantly available to you.

If God knows everything, why pray?

By praying you deepen your friendship with Jesus. But prayer is not just asking for things. Prayer is being with him, sharing things with him. God is almighty. He does know everything. He is in full control and he loves you and cares for you very deeply. Just as a human father likes to hear all that his children have been doing during the day, so our heavenly Father loves to hear all we do – all our hopes and joys, our fears and worries. While he was on earth Jesus prayed to his Father. If he felt the need to pray, how much more should his followers.

He taught us to pray and promises to answer every prayer. Sometimes, though, his answer is 'no', for he knows what is best for us. Wise parents will not always give their children what they ask for. Sometimes the answer is 'wait', for they know it is not yet the right time. Sometimes the answer is a clear 'yes'.

How should I pray?

Prayer should follow naturally from your reading of the Bible. Try to find a quiet place and, if possible, be alone.

Remember. Remember the one to whom you are coming. Sometimes it helps to read a hymn or a psalm such as Psalm 95, 98, 100, 147 or 150. Just enjoy being in his presence. He loves you to come to him in this way.

Confess. We always come to God as people who need forgiveness. Ask him to show you your sins and failings. Ask him to forgive you and to help you overcome them in the future.

Thank. Spend a few minutes thinking of all that you have to thank him for: forgiving your sins; his love for you; the Lord Jesus; the Bible; the Holy Spirit; Christian friends; your family; your health and skills; answered prayer.

Pray for others. Get a small notebook and make a list of people to pray for: your family and friends, leaders in the state and in your church, missionaries. Pray for a few each day. Be definite, don't just make vague requests for God's blessing. As you pray, use your imagination, picture the person and their situation. Pray as you read the newspaper and watch the news.

Pray for yourself. Pray about every aspect of your life: the day ahead, any problems, duties or fears, your witness as a Christian at home and at work, God's will for your life. Talk naturally as to a close friend, but remember, too, that you are in the presence of God himself.

Pray with other Christians. Jesus gives a special promise of answered prayer when just two or three meet in his name to pray. It will also bring you closer to other members of God's family.

Pray at all times. The lines are always open and you can talk to him at any time of the day or night.

What about other religions?

❝ Surely all roads lead to God, so it doesn't matter what you believe or which road you are on as long as you are sincere?❞

Man alone of all creation is a worshipping being. This is perhaps the main difference between man and the rest of the animal world: this inner feeling that there is someone out there greater than him.

Every civilization, every primitive tribe, has had its objects of worship: gods. Usually they are focused on the sun or moon or river or some animal. Always there is a desire to please the gods by offering sacrifices.

Behind it all is our search for God. This search shows itself in many ways in the world's religions.

Hindus try to get away from the world and its evil influences by relaxing the body and the mind and so coming closer to Brahman – their creator god. They aim to achieve this by extreme concentration and meditation helped by the bodily exercises of yoga.

Buddhists see the body as full of evil, but believe it can be overcome by acts of self-denial and self-discipline. Only so can they hope to reach the blessed state of eternal bliss – Nirvana. They therefore believe in an elaborate system of reincarnation to achieve this: coming back into this world again and again, hoping to get better each time.

The Muslim stresses total obedience to the laws of his holy book, the Koran, as the only way to please God. All the great religions of the world have in common:

▎a desire to come to God
▎a desire to live a good and holy life
▎a desire for life after death.

The founders of these religions were all looking for God. Jesus said *he* was God. 'He who has seen me has seen the Father,' he said.

Other religious leaders have pointed the way to God. Jesus said he was the only way to God: 'I am the way, the truth and the life. No one comes to the Father except by me.'

The other religions claim no personal knowledge of God, no certainty of forgiveness of sins or of life after death. They all stress the only way is by trying to get better, trying to obey moral laws and religious rules.

Jesus promises complete forgiveness because of his death for our sins on the cross.

Jesus promises victory over death. He also promises life with him in heaven after death because he rose again.

Jesus promises power in our lives to grow more like him, because he gives the Holy Spirit to all who trust in him.

Being a Christian is not a case of desperately trying to find God. The heart of Christianity is God so loving us that he sent Jesus to find us and bring us into a close and loving relationship with him now in this life and throughout the whole of eternity. Christianity is trusting Jesus and what he did, rather than trusting our good deeds to bring us to God.

Why is there so much suffering?

‹ If God is love why do people suffer so much? Why doesn't he stop it all? ›

This is an impossible question to answer. There is so much in life that is a mystery and we have to admit we don't have the answers. There is so much about God that we cannot even begin to understand, simply because he is far greater in wisdom and power than we are. But as in other dark areas of life, the Bible sheds light. Without faith in God, the whole question of suffering will become a meaningless tangle of knots.

I *Suffering can come because of human sin.* A drunken driver can cause untold pain and suffering to innocent bystanders. The pride and greed of Hitler brought terrible suffering to countless millions of people. When God made us, he gave us the precious gift of free will. It is this that makes us human, enabling us to love and hate, help or hurt others. Without it we would be robots or machines incapable of love. But this great gift of free will has been used again and again for evil. What we do affects other people for good or bad.

I *Suffering can come because of human imperfection.* No man or woman is perfect, and because of this we get ill, grow old and die. This is why deformed children are sometimes born. This is not God's doing. He is not punishing the parents. He does not send illness. Disease and illness are all part of a sinful world and we are all subject to them – Christians as well as others.

I *Suffering can come because of human error.* Hundreds of children were born crippled because their mothers took the Thalidomide drug. No way can God be blamed for this tragedy or others which result from either carelessness or lack of knowledge.

I *Suffering can come because of natural disasters.* In some strange way, sin has affected our earth and it is out of order. Because of this, earthquakes, floods and droughts take place in parts of the world. People living in these areas are constantly open to such disasters.

There are plenty of instances in the Bible of God punishing a wicked nation or person. But God does no send suffering. He allows it as he allowed his only Son to suffer on the cross for our sins. God only acts in love and justice. He cannot do wrong and he never makes mistakes. He can see the end as well as the beginning. We are like people looking at the back of a tapestry: lots of threads all over the place and only a vague idea of the finished picture.

God is not controlled by time. We get angry and disillusioned with God if our prayers are not answered at once and in the way we expect. God does hear and answer, but in his way and in his time. We somehow have a built-in belief that God will always keep us from all accidents and illnesses.

God sometimes allows suffering to test and strengthen the muscles of our faith. The way we react in suffering will determine whether we are growing in faith or slipping back into doubts and resentment. God suffers with us. He comes alongside us, helps us to accept it, live with it and overcome it through his power and our own determination. Suffering brings God's people closer to him. They refuse to be beaten by it, because they know with Jesus that the suffering of the cross was the prelude to Easter Day, and the best is yet to be.

Is there life after death?

The coffin is lowered into the ground, the curtains at the crematorium close. It all seems so final. Can we really believe there is an afterlife? Death is part of belonging to a 'sinful world'.

We can see ourselves in the following way:

I a body: the physical side that we can see
I a mind: the side of us that thinks and responds to the world
I a spirit or soul: the side of us that loves, feels and worships –

our personality, what we are deep down – our real self.

Our body gets old and one day it will die. It will have done the job it was meant to do for our life here. When we die, or rather when our body dies, our spirit lives on because it can never die or be killed. When we go to a funeral and see the coffin, only the body is there. The spirit of the person we knew is not there.

What happens next? To answer this we have to go to the only one with the answer. Jesus went through the experience of death and came back alive, and he alone can speak with authority on life after death. He tells of two eternal worlds: heaven and hell.

Hell is where God has withdrawn his presence and therefore all light and love. Jesus describes it as a place of darkness, weeping and torment. Certain violent criminals are sentenced to life imprisonment. Hell is eternal life imprisonment with no possible remission. In this life God has provided the remission or forgiveness of sins by letting Jesus take that terrible death sentence. God sends no one to hell. People go of their own choice by ignoring or rejecting Jesus as the one hope of freedom and eternal life. The Bible calls this eternal separation from God.

Jesus describes heaven as the true home of all God's people. The Christian does not belong here on earth. We are journeying through this short, passing life to our true home that Jesus is preparing. He will be there. God the Father will be there. The Holy Spirit will be there, so too the angels of God and every one of God's children; all who have loved him and trusted him from the dawn of creation.

Heaven is shown as a place of perfect love and happiness, of lasting peace and complete satisfaction – so lovely and wonderful that we cannot even begin to understand it. There will be no more sin, no death, no evil, no violence or hatred, no grief or partings, no devil to tease and torment, no more pain and suffering.

The Christian's life here is a preparation for that marvellous life to come. We shall see Jesus face to face. We will be raised from death with a new, spiritual body at the end of time. That resurrection body will be just like Jesus' resurrected body, perfectly suited for life with him in heaven. All the puzzles and mysteries of life will be solved.

If you love Jesus you need never be afraid of death. For when your body dies, as some day it will, the real you will go straight to be with Jesus! It will be like falling asleep and then waking up. The first person you will see will be Jesus himself welcoming you home at last.

How will it all end?

Is the human race going to blow itself and this world to pieces?

It is quite true that for the first time in history we have the means to do this. But, whatever people may do, the message of the Bible rings out, 'our God reigns'. God is in control of everything, and nothing that the human race can ever do will stop God's will being done. The day is coming and coming fast when he will be seen to be in complete control.

How will this happen? Jesus made it crystal clear that he would once again break into human history, not as a helpless baby, but as supreme king of all creation, heaven and earth. The Bible is full of this on page after page. It has been the confident hope of Christians down the centuries, based on Jesus' own promise, 'I will come again'. His second coming in power and glory will close the book on human and world history.

❚ *When will this take place?* The simple answer is that we don't know. Only God knows. Jesus did, however, warn us of the signs of his return:

❚ natural disasters, earthquakes and famines

❚ wars and uprisings, revolutions and cruel oppression

❚ Christians suffering fierce persecution

❚ increase in fear and tension, breakdowns in relationships

❚ false sects and false religious leaders springing up.

All this has been partly happening in the past, but never before has it all been happening at once and growing all the time.

Jesus said his return would be sudden. He compared it to a flash of lightning, lighting up a dark sky. He warned that the world would be unprepared. His coming again will be personal. Jesus himself will come, and it will be clearly visible for all to see. He will given total authority over all other powers, human or satanic.

❚ *What will his return be like?* It will mean the end of the world as we know it. Its purpose will have been served. Peter describes it in this way: 'On that day the heavens will disappear with a shrill noise. The heavenly bodies will burn up and be destroyed and the earth with everything in it will vanish.'

Jesus will return as Judge. The whole of mankind will be divided into two – God's people to eternal life – the rest to eternal death. There will be nothing unfair about his judgment. It will be based on what a person in his or her lifetime did with Jesus. That decision will be the basis of what happens in eternity. The choice is ours.

Life as we know it will finish, but a glorious new life is there ready for the children of God; a new heaven and a new earth is ow the new creation is described.

In the light of all this what sort of people should we be? We should be:

ready to meet Jesus at any time

living a life that would not cause us shame should he suddenly appear

using the time wisely by sharing with others the good news of Jesus and growing constantly in faith and love.